MY JOURNEY TO STANFORD

Copyright © 2019 My Journey to Stanford

All rights reserved. No part of this publication may be reproduced in whole or in part, or stored in a retrieval system, or transmitted in any form or by any means, including electronic, mechanical, photocopying, recording, or otherwise, without the prior written permission of the copyright owner.

ISBN-13: 9781727162622

Disclaimer: I am not an admission officer, nor do I claim to know everything about the college admission process. This book is written from my perspective, from what I believe admission officers are looking for. This book represents my opinion, and I cannot guarantee you admission into top-tier universities. Minor adjustments have been made to my application to protect my privacy, including my name. Additionally, facts shift from year to year. By reading this book, you recognize that I cannot be held responsible for your college admission results.

TO MY BROTHER, PETER

CONTENTS

Introduction 7

Part One: My Journey to Palm Drive 13
  Go Behind the Scenes 15
  My Application 39

Part Two: Insights 77
  Extracurricular Activities 79
  Academics 99
  Recommendation Letters 115
  Essays 127

Conclusion 135

Acknowledgements 141

INTRODUCTION

ON MOVE-IN DAY, I watched palm trees stretching towards the sky. I was bumping along with my luggage down Palm Drive, stealing looks out of the car window: Above me was an unending, blue sky, broken up by the billowing leaves of palm trees. In front of me was perhaps the most famous view of Stanford. Memorial Church gleamed in the sunlight, and Main Quad's burgundy roofs and beige walls sprawled, foregrounded by lush grass and backdropped by rolling mountains.

"Take in this view," my mom said to me from the driver's seat. "Not many people can drive down Palm Drive and call it home."

Her words were almost overwhelming. I realized then that the grand view before me, full of hidden futures, rich pasts, tear-joy victories and tragic heartbreaks of all shapes and sizes, was mine to share in. Starting from today, I would shape and be shaped by a place that, a few years ago, seemed only an unreachable, faraway dream.

My path to Stanford was not like the drive down Palm Drive. It was not a breezy, linear journey towards a new home. Instead, it was a winding path. Sometimes I would catch a gush of wind forward. Other times I would try to fly against strong wind currents, only for them to push me back.

In this little book, I will do my best to illuminate my journey to Palm Drive. I will provide a list of my courses and standardized test scores; I will show how I worded my extracurricular activities and awards in the Common Application; I will show what I wrote in the additional information section; and I will share with you my Common Application essay along with my Stanford, MIT, and Yale supplemental essays. This will give you the opportunity to see my whole application, which is an extremely powerful resource. For instance, one can read an essay in isolation from the internet or from other books, and, while those are useful, they pale in comparison to seeing not only how the various essays in a single application interact but also how the essays interact with the application as a whole.

Before sharing with you the application that admission officers saw, I will walk you through how my application came to be. The story behind my academics and extracurriculars. How I went from being the shyest kid in my class to being one of the most active students in my high school. How I started participating in my extracurriculars, and how I built them up year to year.

In this way, I hope to demonstrate that getting into a place like Stanford is doable for those who desire it. I got into Stanford despite being a typical student when I entered high school. When I entered freshman year of high school, I did not have any special talents, as I did not excel at any sport, art, or academic pursuit, and had many B's on my middle school transcript. By writing this book, I want to break down the common misconception that one needs to be hyper-talented in order to get into a university like Stanford. Additionally, I want to demonstrate that it is not the starting point that matters but rather dedication and drive.

In this book, I will also go over the four components that form a college application: extracurricular activities, academics, recommendation letters, and essays. I have a section dedicated to each of these components, where I offer invaluable advice and insights, the stuff I wish I knew when I was applying to college.

Ultimately, this is not a how-to book because there is no how-to to get into a place like Stanford. Rather than offering a step-to-step guide, I offer you my journey so that perhaps you can learn from my successes and failures. I hope that my perspective as a student who has gone through the process and who has succeeded in many ways will provide you with a greater understanding of admissions to top-tier universities. However, I must acknowledge that I am not an admission officer and that I do not know everything. My application, too, was not perfect.

In total, I applied to eight universities. I was accepted into Stanford, MIT, Yale, University of Pennsylvania Wharton, Duke, and University of California, Berkeley, where I was a Regents Scholar and was admitted into their competitive Management, Entrepreneurship, and Technology program. I was rejected from Harvard and Princeton. If you are wondering why I only applied to eight universities, all of which are highly competitive, it is because I applied to Stanford in the Restricted Early Action round and was accepted. Thus, I knew about my acceptance to Stanford by December. Because of this, I withdrew my application from other universities that I knew I would not attend over Stanford in order to make space for other applicants.

I wrote most of this book the summer before my first year at Stanford, in the gentle and warm sun of my hometown in California. I hope you have something to gain from reading it, whether that be an inspiration to start a personal project, a commitment towards building a relationship with a teacher, an essay idea, a spark about how to write about your activities on the Common Application, the introspection to recognize the little desires that tug on your heart, the courage to do something that may not succeed, or a firm faith that you can get into top-tier universities if you set your heart to it.

PART ONE:

My Journey to Palm Drive

GO BEHIND THE SCENES

BEFORE I GO into my actual application, I want to give you insight into the life that eventually gave shape to my application. In this way, when you later read my application, you will have a fuller understanding of the person and story behind it.

Perhaps, the biggest takeaway from this section is that there wasn't one big revelation, one big transformation that catapulted me to Stanford. Instead, it was a slow, gradual process. I started someplace small and slowly climbed up from there.

My detailed journey to Stanford is far more complex than the space I have to articulate it. Here, I pick out the most essential components. I believe my story starts with this—overcoming tears.

OVERCOMING TEARS

I remember my first day of high school clearly. Fumbling my way through hallways with classrooms numbered in ways I did not understand, a crumbled map stretched between my two hands, I finally stumbled my way into my first period math class. I can picture myself then, tangled hair bouncing against my backpack, breath heavy from stress and nervousness, as I sought for the courage to open to door to the unknown. Little did I know then that I was opening the door to a transformation, that, in a matter of years, I would go from the shy, unknown, mediocre, middle school student to a well-known leader and student.

But my journey to Stanford started long before I emerged from my cocoon on the first day of high school. It actually started when I was five years old, as I stood in front of my first grade classroom. My parents were there with me, and, in my terror, I refused to leave them. I clung to them, tears streaming down my face, and my first grade teacher had to pry me away. In fact, it was like this every morning for two whole weeks. This was because I was a painfully shy kid. Tears were my way of expressing timidity. This same kind of fear followed me not just to school but also to the classes my parents signed me up for, like piano and sports. Because of this, I never excelled at any of them.

However, I am lucky to have parents who were attuned to my weaknesses. For instance, when I was eight, my parents signed me up to sing at the local library talent show. I was not an amazing singer by any standards, but my parents decided it would be beneficial for me to sing in front of a public audience. Upon hearing the news, I simply dismissed it. The answer was simple: I would refuse to sing. However, as the talent show approached, it became clear that my parents were not backing down.

The day came with much anxiety, but, eventually, I made it up on the stage and sang to a group of forty people. As I was singing, I looked out at the audience members; they were listening intently and giving me encouraging nods. In those moments, I remember feeling special—the feeling of being heard, seen. After my performance, my parents congratulated me and told me how beautiful my voice was and how engrossed the audience members were. Never mind if their words were true—they gave me confidence. Because of their positive encouragement, just a few months later, I was able to sing in front of hundreds of people. To this day, I am amazed by my younger self's ability to scale stages and to sing boldly to large audiences without paralyzing fear.

Because of those experiences, I was undaunted by crowds. However, I continued to be shy. I would come to occupy a duality that would follow me to high school; I was both shy and loud, both quiet and outspoken, both an introvert and a leader. When I started middle school, I signed up for the debate team. I am not sure what drove me to join, but my experiences singing to audiences showed me that debate was not something to be afraid of, despite the fact that many of my classmates were too daunted to join. Debate was a bumpy ride: I experienced tears when a judge judged me harshly, laughter when I messed up so hard the only thing I could do was laugh, and genuine joy when my team and I did well at a tournament. Debate was a formative experience for me. It helped me see holes in arguments, anticipate refutations, and speak without a script in front of me. It also introduced me to the competitive debate scene, which I would continue to be a part of in high school. Debate served as the stepping stone for many accomplishments that helped me get into Stanford, such as my speech and debate awards, my award-winning business pitches, and my leadership positions. So while I may not have emerged from the middle school debate team as an amazing debater, it helped shape me and gave me so much more than just debate itself.

READING USELESS BOOKS

During middle school, I engaged in one other significant activity outside of debate and academics, and that was reading young adult fiction novels, like *The Hunger Games* and *The Fault in Our Stars*. While I did not read much in elementary school, I became obsessed with these books in middle school, as they were full of giddy romances, suspense, tragedy, and the beautiful, messy transition from innocence to maturity. Eating breakfast while quickly devouring the words on the page was one of my favorite moments in the day.

My parents always encouraged me to read more substantial novels, like *Animal Farm* or *Pride and Prejudice*, the classics that, unlike young adult novels, would improve my reading comprehension and vocabulary. Upon seeing me read the romance, dystopian novel *Matched,* my mother commented, "What a useless book. Read something that's better for you." In some sense, my mother had a point: reading young adult novels did not improve my English ability significantly. However, if I were to do it all over again, I would still go back to those same books and fall in love with their characters and language because they gave me something I would continue to cherish for the rest of my life: an interest in writing.

Reading so much young adult fiction inspired me to write my own novel. I spent many of my middle school years writing, one word, one chapter at a time. Eventually, I wrote a seventy-five thousand word novel that I would continually revisit and rewrite even throughout high school. Honestly, it was not a particularly good novel, and I never published it or anything, but it gave me the knowledge that I can pursue and complete long-term projects, that, while the goal may be daunting, taking things one step at a time, one word after another, will guide me to the finish line. It taught me that there is beauty in pursuing fields that are not my strength, taught me that hard work and drive are infinitely more important than talent, and most importantly taught me the value of language and literature. Reading young adult fiction also inspired me to write short stories; it led me to write this very book you're reading and encouraged me to take creative writing courses at Stanford. Sometimes, doing the "useless" thing, if done out of genuine passion, can lead one to beautiful places.

22

CHOOSING A HIGH SCHOOL

Students at my middle school typically went to private high schools. My parents wanted me to follow this tradition; they wanted me to stay clear of our neighborhood's public high school, as it had a low Academic Performance Index (API) score and was notorious for drug and alcohol use.

During the last week of eighth grade, my English teacher asked us to share our high school acceptances to the class. Each student went in turn, and one after the other I heard names of selective high schools rolling off of my classmates' tongues followed by modest smiles. When it got to me, I peeped out the name of a high school that was not as desirable as others in the area, and a wave of embarrassment washed over me. But the moment was fleeting; the teacher quickly moved on to the next student, who continued the pattern of naming prestigious high schools.

I had applied to a handful of private high schools around the Bay Area and was rejected by all but one, the one that, at the time, accepted a significant portion of their applicants.

My parents debated about sending me there, as their research told them that each year the high school boasted two national merit semifinalists maximum, and, while we heard of students getting into universities like UCLA and Rice, we had not heard of anyone getting into universities like Stanford and Yale, although this would change in the next few years. However, getting into a top-tier university was not one of my parents' goals for me, not because they did not care but because they did not believe their daughter who got B's on her report card and who sometimes got in trouble with the principal could get into a place like Stanford. So, in the end, they decided to send me to the private high school despite their reservations.

FRESHMAN YEAR

I remember feeling shocked, thinking *uh-oh*, feeling my heart sinking while I sat in my first Biology Honors class. I had just heard my teacher (who was over six feet tall and pregnant, and still wore high-heeled shoes which clanked aggressively against the tiled floor) tell our class that we would have quizzes every class, tests that spanned multiple chapters of the textbook, and finals that weighed significantly on our final grade. I wondered if I could even survive the class.

I remember feeling overwhelmed. I arrived at the high school gym for club fair, where I came upon rows upon rows of tables and club posters, the constant sound of shouting, of shoes against shiny gym floors. I was drawn to everything, seeing all the cool things one can do in high school, and intimidated by everything. I was wondering where I would find my place, if I ever would. Naturally, I signed up to be a part of my high school's speech and debate team. I also signed up for robotics and DECA (a business club), and decided to participate in a school-wide business competition.

I remember feeling nervous, walking into the first speech and debate meeting, knowing no one, and I remember feeling shocked to find only ten members. The team was small, and I learned Parliamentary Debate was the only debate form the team participated in, an impromptu debate form where teams are given only twenty minutes to prepare the case. The upperclassmen there seemed seasoned and intimidating. I knew I had a lot to learn.

There are three divisions in debate: Varsity, JV, and Novice. Despite my former debate experience, I started off in the Novice division, since high school debate is a whole different ballgame than middle school debate. At my first tournament, my partner and I went 2-3, meaning two wins and three loses. At our next tournament, we went undefeated. From then on, we competed in the JV division and did mediocre for the rest of the year.

I spent most of my time in robotics, actually. During the busiest season, I spent around 20 hours a week. However, I did not rejoin robotics my sophomore year because it took up a significant amount of time and because I did not find myself enjoying the time I spent in the robotics lab. It was not an easy decision, as I had sunk so much time and energy into it; I practically altered my whole schedule so that I could make time for it. At the end of the day, however, I am glad I left robotics behind to pursue activities I was more passionate about.

Aside from robotics, I participated in a school-wide business competition. I did not have any prior exposure to business, but I decided to give it a try. As part of the competition, we were tasked to come up with a business idea and pitch it to a panel of judges. I partnered with two other freshmen and was the "CEO" of my team. My team ended up winning. The true prize of winning was not winning itself but rather the confidence it gave me. It showed me that I had the capability of leading a team, that I could achieve greatly if I put my heart into it.

Overall, my freshman year was about finding footing. I joined clubs and I quit them. I won and I lost. In truth, I was not seriously committed to any of my extracurriculars. I did not do anything that would be get-into-Stanford worthy, but freshman year set the ground-work for my success in my later high school years. A year of all A's, a first-place win at a business competition, and the warmth of the debate team gave me reassurance that high school was doable, that I could knock it out of the park if I wanted to.

SOPHOMORE YEAR

Sophomore year was the year that propelled me to the next level, both academically and extracurricularly. The feeling of success during my freshman year drove me to take a fairly heavy course load compared to my peers, as I was one of three or four students in my grade who took four AP classes that year. As a result, many of my classmates in classes such as AP Statistics and AP Physics 1 were one or two grades older than me. While this may seem to put me at a disadvantage, it was actually inspiring and gave me the opportunity to form friendships and connections with students who were further ahead on their educational journey.

In fact, one of those classes, AP Statistics, was particularly formative for me. That class was filled with upperclassmen who asked intelligent questions, and I had a teacher who encouraged me to think critically rather than to memorize. That class sparked in me a sort of intellectual spirit that I would carry with me throughout the rest of high school. It taught me to think actively, to compare what the teacher said in class to my own understanding—and if the two did not match up, I would ask the teacher questions to clarify. I found myself asking questions with the same level of intellectualism that those in my AP Statistics class asked—and I believe this, more than anything, my grades and test scores included, is what separated me academically from all the other top students in my grade.

From the previous year, I continued doing debate and DECA. I started competing in the Varsity division for debate, and while I did not win any awards in Parliamentary Debate, I won a major competition in Impromptu Speaking. I was shocked when I found out the news, so shocked, in fact, that I did not even stay for the award ceremony afterward because it did not cross my mind that I would end up winning the tournament. What I can say, however, is that I came into the tournament prepared. I had spent weeks thinking of stories; in the blank, empty moments of my day, I would run my mind around the contours of the stories I wanted to tell, thinking of the best way to shape them, to give them their power. In Impromptu Speaking, one does not know the topic beforehand, but, at the core of it, regardless of the topic, are stories, and from my middle school years I had an ocean of stories that I thought were beautiful. What I knew then was that if I thought a story was beautiful, the judges would, too; they would be able to feel it from my delivery.

In addition, infused with knowledge from the business competition in my freshman year, I competed well at DECA competitions. I won 3rd place at the California State DECA conference in the Start-up Business Plan category, which qualified me for the International DECA competition, where I won 6th place. To write of this accomplishment takes only five lines, which belies the energy and time I poured into it. What I learned about DECA was that the victory goes to the individual who spends the most amount of productive time and puts in the most thought into the project. There is no secret other than constant dedication and bit of creativity.

Beyond continuing the extracurricular activities of my freshman year, I started doing two new activities. First, in my freshman year, I took a class called "Introduction to Engineering Design," where I learned how to use Autodesk Inventor and 3D printers. Fascinated by the ability to create something of my own design, I started the 3D Design club at my high school in the beginning of my sophomore year, where each week during lunch, I, along with my teammates, taught the basics of 3D design to the club members. In addition to teaching, we volunteered for an organization called Enabling the Future, and through them we 3D printed prosthetic hands for children missing fingers.

Second, inspired by my AP Computer Science class, I started to compete in the USA Computing Olympiad, which consists of a series of four-hour programming contests that test critical thinking and creativity. In order to solidify my skills in programming, I took an informal algorithms class outside of school, and, by the end of the year, I made it to the Gold Division.

Sophomore year crystallized me as one of my grade's top students: I took four AP classes and received high AP scores—three fives and one four—and sophomore year taught me how to be an active student in class. This, coupled with my achievements in speech, DECA, and programming, and the satisfaction of leading my own club, set up the foundation for my acceptance into Stanford.

JUNIOR YEAR

Junior year I tried to take everything up a notch, pushing past boundaries and into new territory. For example, my academic course load intensified, as I started to take five challenging AP classes. Additionally, I poured effort into activities such as debate and computer programming so that I could improve. However, while I was working on taking my academics and extracurricular activities to the next level, my time spent working on them did not increase significantly, as I was building off of the strong foundation of my freshman and sophomore years and because I started to get a grasp of spending my time efficiently.

During the summer before my junior year, I participated in the Secondary Student Training Program (SSTP), a residential, five-and-a-half week research program at the University of Iowa. Students participated in research across different disciplines in STEM. I specifically worked at a Computer Science lab, where I conducted independent research on the convergence of the PageRank algorithm.

Once school started, I continued participating in debate and DECA and leading the 3D Design club. I was elected to leadership positions in debate and DECA. In debate, my partner and I made elimination rounds at a major tournament for the first time, and because of that we were given a debate ranking. In an effort to boost our ranking, we went to more tournaments and did relatively well at them. At our peak, we were ranked 23rd in the nation. I also worked hard on my DECA report. At the California State DECA competition, my team tied for 4th in the Public Relations Campaign category, but we did not qualify for the International DECA competition.

I continued competing in the USA Computing Olympiad and made it to the Platinum Division, the highest division. This distinction significantly helped my application, especially for MIT. It showed that I could problem-solve at a high level.

Finally, I applied to be a youth commissioner of my city and was appointed. As a youth commissioner, I wrote policy recommendations to City Council; organized youth-related, city-wide conferences; spoke at various conferences and rallies; and started the Through Teens' Eyes project in an effort to better understand teens in my city. The goal of this project was to publish a collection of personal stories representing the challenges, feelings, and experiences of youth. By my senior year, the project was completed, and my teammates and I successfully self-published the book on Amazon. I believe that this project significantly helped my application. It showed my initiative, leadership, and dedication towards giving voice to the voiceless. It showed my humanity, that I genuinely care about the lives and experiences of others. Additionally, it might seem from this description that the project was effortlessly done, but in reality, I—along with my teammates—ran into a lot of challenges and spent a lot of blood, sweat, and tears getting this project off the ground. Seeing this project from start to finish was a rewarding experience.

Overall, junior year was a stressful year: I had a hard time boosting my SAT English score past the 700-730 range, and the pressure of 6 AP exams (English, US History, Calculus, Spanish, Physics Mechanics, Physics E&M) loomed around the corner. But when I checked my AP exam scores—all fives—I knew I had a real shot of getting into America's top universities.

SENIOR YEAR

The summer before my senior year, I participated in the Stanford Institutes of Medicine Summer Research Program (SIMR), a highly selective research program; in my year, the acceptance rate was around 6%. I believe I got accepted because of my previous research experience at SSTP and because of the USA Computing Olympiad Platinum Division award. Similar to SSTP, each student is assigned to a lab and works under the guidance of a mentor, usually a post-doc or a grad student. In my case, I interned at a bioinformatics lab, where I used R to analyze autopsy data.

Senior year, I continued the extracurricular activities that I participated in my junior year. I was elected as Chair of the youth commission.

I spent most of my days catching up on *Grey's Anatomy* episodes and writing college applications, which took more time than I expected.

The first semester of senior year was simultaneously relaxed and stressful. While I had a lot of free time in my day, the looming college application deadlines were a constant stressor. Once they were over, however, I had the best time I ever had in high school.

THE DOMINO EFFECT

A line of dominos. Suddenly, a drive, a gush of wind. A domino stumbles, falls—then, the whole line starts tumbling, one after the other.

I believe it is vital to understand how things add up. How big sweeping changes do not just happen. How they are grown out of small disturbances. One domino at a time. Maybe my application, or other applications that you've seen, seem impossible to you, but one does not have to be superhuman to have an application worthy of top-tier universities. Rather, one needs to create little disturbances here and there, to fight off the inertia, so that the first domino can be knocked down. Then, allow your achievements to add up; view them as means rather than as ends, and the results can be staggering.

Here, I want to show you how one activity led me to the next. How I started off somewhere simple and slowly escalated into a place that opened doors to top-tier universities. I bolded areas that significantly strengthened my application.

1. Computer Science to Biomedical Research

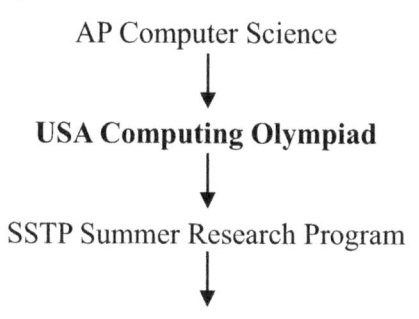

AP Computer Science
↓
USA Computing Olympiad
↓
SSTP Summer Research Program
↓
Stanford Institutes of Medicine Summer Research Program

2. The Impact of Middle School Debate

Middle School Debate
↓
Good Speaking Abilities
↙ ↓ ↘

Winner of the school-wide business competition
↓
DECA + other business awards
↓
LaunchX Regional Director

Participation in high school debate
↓
A year competing in the debate Varsity division as a sophomore
↓
National ranking in Parliamentary debate in junior year

Youth Commission Appointment
↓
Through Teens' Eyes + speaking engagements at rallies and conferences

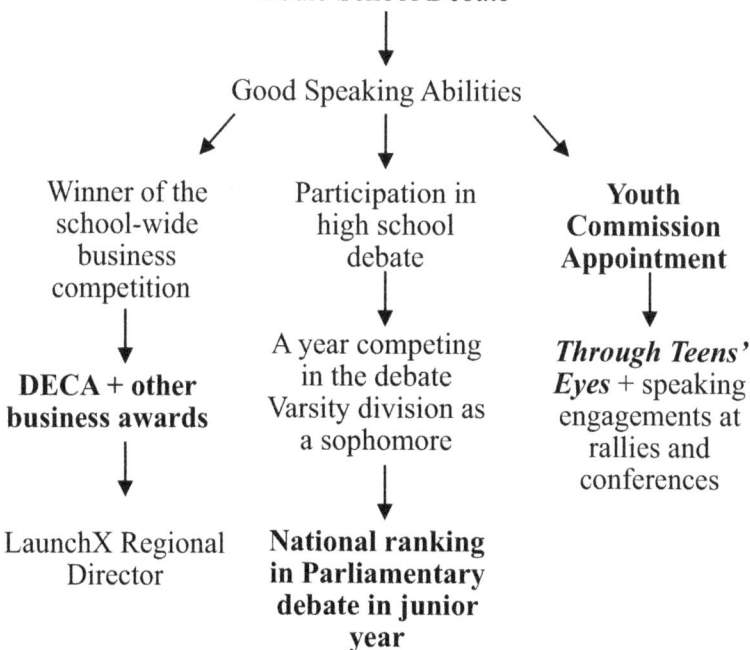

37

MY APPLICATION

COURSEWORK

Subject	9	10	11	12
Math	Algebra 2 H	Trig/ Precalculus H	AP Calculus BC	Multivariable Calculus H
Science	Biology H	AP Physics 1	AP Physics C	AP Biology
English	English 9 H	English 10 H	AP English Language	AP English Literature
History		AP Human Geography	AP US History	AP Micro Econ / AP US Gov
Foreign Language	Spanish 2	Spanish 4	AP Spanish Langauge	
Business / Tech	Intro to Engineering Design	AP Computer Science	Intro to Entrepreneurship	Advanced Business H
Elective	Physical Education	AP Statistics		Student Government
Elective	Wind Ensemble			

By receiving A's and A+'s in a schedule packed with AP and honors classes, I showed admission officers that I was a highly capable student. My high school did not rank students officially, but unofficially I was in the top 1% of my class.

STANDARDIZED TESTING

Exam	Grade Taken	Score
AP Statistics	10	5
AP Physics 1	10	4
AP Computer Science	10	5
AP Human Geography	10	5
AP English Language	11	5
AP US History	11	5
AP Spanish Language	11	5
AP Physics C: Mechanics	11	5
AP Physics C: E&M	11	5
AP Calculus BC	11	5
SAT (1st time)	11	730 (E), 790 (M)
SAT (2nd time)	11	760 (E), 790 (M)
SAT II Math	10	800
SAT II Physics	11	800
SAT II US History	11	760

ACTIVITIES

Here is how I described my activities on the Common Application. For reference, I applied as a Computer Science major for most schools.

Description	Grade
SIMR - Research Intern at Stanford Constructed a landscape of organ-specific immunity to investigate the impacts of organ, sex & aging on the immune system using R programming lang.	12, Summer
Computer Science Research Intern at Univ. of Iowa Developed a search engine in Python. Conducted research on the performance of various implementations of the PageRank algorithm.	11, Summer
Chair of the Youth Commission Represent 250K youth. Advise Mayor & City Council. Write policy recommendations. Organize youth motivational conference. Lead Youth Advisory Council.	11 - 12

MIT LaunchX USA West Regional Director Organized 1st US West Pitch Event. Recruit mentors. Form partnerships.	11 - 12
Founder and President of 3D Design Teach 3D printing and CAD weekly. Make prosthetic hands for kids. 3D printed customized items for those in need.	10 - 12
Vice President of Speech and Debate Mentor teams. Instructed Parli debate & diff speech formats. Propelled VCHS into a nationally ranked HS -1st time top 30. Coached summer debate camp.	9 - 12
DECA Board of Dir (12), Dir of Competition (11) Mentor officers. Set vision & strategies. Instructed DECA members (60+) on competition materials. Tripled ICDC (International) qualifiers.	9 - 12
Speaker at Summits & Conferences Encourage teens to protect the environment & to be involved. Speak to adults on parenting & on the impact of marijuana on teens and the environment.	11 - 12

44

| Varsity tennis player | 9 - 11 |

Organized team bonding events, such as Secret Sister and Senior Night. We played and cheered our hearts out.

AWARDS

Here are the awards I listed under the "awards" section of the Common Application. A maximum of five awards can be listed. If one desires to list more than five awards, the "additional information" section of the Common Application is a great place to do that.

Award	Scope	Grade
USACO (USA Computing Olympiad) Platinum Division Competitor	National	11
Nationally Ranked 23rd in Parliamentary Debate at my peak	National	11
ICDC (DECA International) Start-up Business Plan 6th place	International	10
1st Place Columbia University Model Entrepreneur Competition	National	11
1st Place Santa Clara University Spring Invitational Open Impromptu Speaking	National	10

ADDITIONAL INFORMATION

Additional information on activities listed:

Speaker

—Youth Empowerment Summit, SF (2017) on how to protect the environment and how to create political change.

—Marijuana Awareness Conference, San José (2017) on the impact of marijuana on the environment.

—World Journal Spring Education Expo (2017) to adults about my perspective on parenting.

—Western Region Robotics Forum, Santa Clara (2015) on entrepreneurship to robotics mentors and students.

Youth Commission Chair

—Organized *Through Teens' Eyes*, an anthology of personal stories from teens throughout the Silicon Valley. *Through Teens' Eyes* is published on amazon.com.

—Responsible for efficient operation of the commission, ensuring each commissioner, liaison, and committee are fulfilling their responsibilities in a timely manner.

—Head of the Environment Ad Hoc Committee

—Organized the Intersections Conference. The conference goal is to encourage youth to embrace the diversity of our city through guest speakers, workshops, and a *Shark-Tank*-style competition.

3D Design
—Partnered with Enabling The Future to 3D print prosthetic hands for children in need.
—Delivered 3D printed keepsakes to comfort hospitalized patients.
—Collaborated with the Missions program to deliver 3D printed crosses to children in Haiti.
—Spearheaded the 1st annual 3D Design Competition. Entrants are tasked with designing something interesting and practical to help others.

SSTP (Secondary Student Training Program) at the University of Iowa
—Best Peer Reviewer Award for asking the most insightful questions.

Additional awards:
Speech and Debate (Varsity/Open Division)
Parliamentary Debate
—4th Place Vikings Invitational (National, 11)
—Quarterfinalist (top 8) at Santa Clara University Fall Invitational (National, 11)
—1st Place Coast Forensics League Tournament (Regional, 11)
—Octofinalist (top 16) at Stephen Stewart Invitational (National, 11)

Speech
—Semifinalist for Original Oratory at Santa Clara University Fall Invitational (National, 10)
—Octofinalist for Impromptu Speaking at Cal Berkeley Invitational (National, 10)

Business
—University of Delaware Diamond Challenge Semifinalist (International, 10)
—DECA California State: 3rd Place Start-Up Business Plan (10); 4th Place Public Relations Campaign (11)

Academic
—Physics Bowl Champion (Team Division) Regional (11)
—Two-time silver key winner of the Scholastic Arts & Writing Contest short story category (10)
—5th Place in Statistics at Santa Clara Valley Math Association Field Day (10)
—National Merit Scholarship Semifinalist (12)
—National AP Scholar (12)

COMMON APPLICATION PERSONAL ESSAY

Discuss an accomplishment, event, or realization that sparked a period of personal growth and a new understanding of yourself or others. (250 - 650 words)

"... forever."

Seventy-five thousand words later, it ended in a quiet roar.

I leaned back against my chair. Amidst swirling feelings, I found fulfillment: I accomplished what I set out to do, one word, one page, one chapter at a time. Three years earlier, I dreamed of writing a novel that could arouse readers to experience a wide spectrum of human emotions. Although I finished the novel, it was not the mature, literary, emotionally-wringing piece I had hoped to create.

A few weeks later, I stayed after class to talk to my English teacher about Ray Bradbury's *Fahrenheit 451*. "I want to write like that."

Casually, she asked, "Are you a writer?" She continued counting the papers on her desk. I shifted my feet. "I write, but I'm not a writer."

Despite the less-than-Bradbury-esque outcomes, I still wanted to write. Everywhere I went, so did my green notebook. It was there as I biked across the city, experiencing the vibrant life around me, my dog jumping in the basket. I carried my notebook as I hiked through Yosemite, rode on buses to tennis matches, and cheered during football games. Whether in a coffee shop or under the blankets at night, I wrote, yearning to stir people's hearts.

In order to create a safe space where teens can write about their experiences without fear of judgement, I started the Through Teens' Eyes Project as a Youth Commissioner. I hoped that readers, young and old, would feel the depth of teens' humanity through these breathing stories.

Members of the youth advisory council sat in a circle, taking turns reading aloud the project submissions. We read a story of a girl grappling with depression, of another defending the significance behind her hijab, and of a teen rejecting a $100 bill from her gambling-addicted father. These stories were the candid voices of imperfect people, helping me see that a moving story quivers with authenticity.

With this insight, I leafed through my old novel. I saw that my sculpted heroine Lillian Heights never erred and that I had constructed a parallel universe in which events unraveled in the best possible way. Perhaps, this was my way of instinctively shielding myself from the struggles of everyday life. So as I began draft three of my novel, I took down my blinders, stepped out of my cocoon of comfort, and started to write about the difficulties I saw. I realized that something beautiful arises from difficult situations: people reaching out in human kindness and empathy. The dedication of a teacher, the compassion of a stranger, the transformation of someone from vengeful to compassionate make these stories—in real life and in fiction—so powerful and moving. As I now run toward, not away from, the realities people face, I find myself being a loyal friend to someone who had once faced despair, helping my little brother stand up to middle school bullying, and conversing with a homeless man about his past. These actions strengthen my feelings of connection to people in every walk of life. We are all heroes, not in the form of knights in shining armor or wizards in invisible cloaks, but rather in the form of ordinary, imperfect human beings.

As I sit in front of the computer screen, I do not wonder if tonight will be the night I write a story worthy of Bradbury. Facing the world head-on, I continue to write, one word after another, digging into a bit more of what is hard, human, and true, hoping that my words reach out and touch someone's heart.

I am a writer.

STANFORD SUPPLEMENTAL ESSAYS

Virtually all of Stanford's undergraduates live on campus. Write a note to your future roommate that reveals something about you or that will help your roommate -- and us -- know you better. (100 to 250 words)

roomie!

i'm super excited to meet you in a few weeks! how are you doing? i'm writing from yosemite. my friends and family just finished a game of cards, and now, i'm under the stars and just spotted the andromeda galaxy with my binoculars.

i know this is quite antiquated—the whole fountain pen on card in an envelope thing, but i'm a huge fan of snail mail: the letters seem more meaningful, and i don't have to worry about google docs or word passive aggressively trying to capitalize my words. with e.e. cummings by my side, i fight them anyway: rebellious i feel.

when we meet, you'll notice that i like to make my own things: lotion, thank you cards brought to life by my calligraphy pen, and even words. maybe we'll experience blitzentente (n.)—the feeling that you deeply understand someone you just met.

my side of the room will be plastered with post-its: quotes i love, spontaneous ideas. add to the collage if you like. on my desk, there will be 3d printed items i designed, like halloween decorations and puzzles i invented. try to solve one if you dare!

    i also collect playing cards. speed, frog, bridge— name the game, and i'll play it with you. if you need chips for a poker game in the dorm, look no further: i got them. small stakes only please.

    i look forward to all the adventures we'll have together!

Tell us about something that is meaningful to you and why. (100 to 250 words)

    Pouring out my heart makes me feel alive.

    Speaking to an audience about a subject I am passionate about is one of the most meaningful experiences I have ever had. On my feet, while I pepper my sentences with humor when the atmosphere feels tense or lower my voice to emphasize a point, everything fades, and it is just the audience and me. I do not speak to tell people what to do. I speak in order to share my perspective, to start a conversation.

    Ultimately, no matter how passionate I am with pathos or reasonable I am with logos, I cannot make people walk the extra ten feet to recycle or turn off the light after everyone else leaves the room. I can only encourage them to care. So I create moments with the audience: I pause, look them in the eye a little longer than I am supposed to, and suddenly, a strong, unexplainable connection is created. These brief moments, I believe, allow my points to resonate with the audience.

After my talk, people begin to discuss my arguments. Members of the audience come up to me and ask questions ranging from, "What steps should I take to start an environmental club at my school?" to "What should I do about my son's video game addiction?"

To speak is to step into the unknown, to create moments in which connection is created, in hopes that my words kindle passion.

What is the most significant challenge that society faces today? (50 word limit)

The Tragedy of the Commons: Our natural inclination towards immediate self-gratification rather than the long-term good of the whole exacerbates world-wide problems such as global warming, obesity, the mushrooming US debt, and sparse retirement savings.

How did you spend your last two summers? (50 word limit)

Hiked to Glacier Point in Yosemite; dove near the Great Barrier Reef; conducted bioinformatics/CS research; organized the city-wide Intersections Conference; befriended brilliant scientists; trained my puppy; screamed at indie/

alternative concerts; taught debate camp; played tennis; invented card games; designed cool/practical objects, like a versatile iEverything stand for my mom.

What historical moment or event do you wish you could have witnessed? (50 word limit)
    I could not just stand there, behind the glass window, watching. If the door was locked, my seven years of martial arts would come in handy, and, breaking the glass, I would storm in and tell Truman what he did not know then about the effects of the nuclear bomb.

What five words best describe you?
    Philomath, activist, ambivert, inventive, inquisitive

When the choice is yours, what do you read, listen to, or watch? (50 word limit)
    TED Talks - Adichie's "The danger of a single story" is my favorite. // *Shark Tank* - Greiner's enthusiasm toward helping budding entrepreneurs inspires me. // Stack Overflow - for CS students, it is a godsend. // *New York Times*, www.dictionaryofobscuresorrows.com, *Never Let Me Go* (book), *Bajo La Misma Estrella* (book), Aquilo (alternative duo)

Name one thing you are looking forward to experiencing at Stanford. (50 word limit)

Learning and designing solutions to world-wide problems at the d.school. Here, in between order and chaos, in the orientation-less rooms teeming with empathy, collaboration, and interdisciplinary study, I can apply my knowledge of computer science and mechanical engineering to develop novel solutions to social problems.

MIT SUPPLEMENTAL ESSAYS

Please tell us more about your cultural background and identity in the space below (100 word limit).

I come from a culture where problems are seen as opportunities. My room is lined with board games and puzzles. My phone teems with logic games like "Unblock Me" and "ExtremeBlock." To me, there is nothing more fascinating than solving, than discovery. I relish elegant solutions to those fiendishly difficult algorithmic problems, and I love the moment when I see a problem in a slightly different light and the pieces start coming together like a jigsaw puzzle. I love delving deeper and deeper in, one step leading to another, solving what initially seemed impossible: I am a problem solver.

We know you lead a busy life, full of activities, many of which are required of you. Tell us about something you do simply for the pleasure of it (100 word limit).

I curate playlists. Many of them are weirdly named, like "SOULS, sir, need room for breathing, for fire." They all capture specific emotion—everything from party-mode to nostalgia.

My playlists are in demand at sports practices when everyone jams to throw-back Taylor Swift and One Direction.

I make playlists for spontaneous drives through San Francisco, and we sing, wind whipping through our hair.

I scream at indie and alternative concerts with total strangers, sing off-key to Spanish music with my family, and swap playlists with my friends. It is the community, which surrounds the music, that I love.

Although you may not yet know what you want to major in, which department or program at MIT appeals to you and why? (100 word limit)

From coding video games in middle school to creating matrices that represent the structure of the Internet, I have always felt the urge to create, to assemble a creative order amidst the growing entropy. As an aspiring entrepreneur, I want to immerse myself into MIT's strong entrepreneurial, hacking, and collaborative culture. Here, a major in computer science will help me gain the technical background to invent innovative products, and a minor in management will give me the skill set to grow a startup into a successful company that changes people's lives.

At MIT, we bring people together to better the lives of others. MIT students work to improve their communities in different ways, from tackling the world's biggest challenges to being a good friend. Describe one way in which you have contributed to your community, whether in your family, the classroom, your neighborhood, etc. (*) (200-250 words)

It was sophomore year, and I had just started the 3D Design Club. I jumped up and down at club fair, holding a flamboyant sign in one hand and a 3D-printed prosthetic hand in the other. "Join the 3D Design Club!" I shouted.

But I didn't just want to create a club. I wanted to create a community, a zone in between order and chaos where practicality and foolishness intertwine.

I try to coach members to be not only better designers but also better innovators. When members first design things, they tend to stick to perceived notions of how something should look or work. So I show them a 3D printed puzzle cube I designed, but it is also a stationery organizer. You can open up each piece and put in staples, paper clips, and mechanical pencil lead. During my three years of leading this club, I've seen members design everything from bookstands that curl up as a dragon's back to triangular marble mazes that grow upwards.

To me, design is about empathy and human connection. We make inanimate objects. But we're making these objects for emotional, sentient human beings. We worked together to design a heart-shaped box for hospitalized patients; in every object, we add meaning by inscribing the recipient's name and engraving a quote or bible verse that relates to the recipient's situation.

Today, my school teems with designers, who now know how to turn their dreams into reality.

Describe the world you come from; for example, your family, clubs, school, community, city, or town. How has that world shaped your dreams and aspirations?(*) (200-250 words)

I cheer on the top of my lungs under the night sky. Only, I can't hear my own voice: It is enveloped in sound, from whistles blowing, cow bells ringing, and the passionate cry, "A couch is not a home!" Signs in hand, green glow sticks haloing on our heads, the fifty of us walk to raise awareness for youth homelessness.

I grew up in the Silicon Valley, in an active and dynamic community full of problem solvers, risk takers, and initiative takers. Here, there is a stark contrast between those who surf the wave of technology and those who are left behind. Living within this fast-paced, technology-driven world has taught me to raise my voice and immediately do something about the problems I see, but it has also taught me to stop and listen--to listen deeply not only with my ears but also with my heart--to the voices that I wouldn't have heard if I had zipped past and averted my eyes to the problems people face. So while I give keynote speeches on protecting the environment, I also take time to interview strangers about their stance on city initiatives and listen to the concerns of residents.

I dream to be an entrepreneur who develops technological solutions to address the prevalent problems in our society. And I dream to touch the lives around me by inspiring others with my words and actions.

YALE SUPPLEMENTAL ESSAYS

*Note that some of the essays here are repeats from before. I reused essays for many schools. I reprint the essays here to give you a sense of what I sent to Yale.

What three areas of study listed below interest you? Why do these areas appeal to you? (100 words or fewer)

I have always felt the urge to create, to problem solve. Studying CS will help me gain the technical skill set to invent innovative products.

Understanding economics allows me to see the world through a different lens; I want to better understand how our individual actions shape the whole and how one event trickles down to affect many others.

I want to feel human rawness seeping from words. To read and to write in one of the most beautiful languages in the world—that is breathing.

What is it about Yale that has led you to apply? (125 words or fewer)

The close-knit, collaborative, and caring community at Yale drew me in immediately. "The professors run the extra mile—all the time," an alum told me. As I walked across the beautiful campus, I could picture myself being a part of YEI, debating about the carbon tax in the dining hall, and frantically reading the Blue Book, unable to choose between trying out an acting class, Infinity, and economics with Robert Shiller. Ultimately, the factor I value most in a school is the people. I long to be a part of the active, dynamic, passionate, and supportive Yale student body.

What inspires you? (35 words or fewer)

Conversations—anything from a friendly debate to a philosophical conversation—not only with people but also with books, movies, and my own mind.

Yale's residential colleges regularly host intimate conversations with guests representing a wide range of experiences and accomplishments. What person, past or present, would you invite to speak? What question would you ask? (35 words or fewer)

Pierre de Fermat: What is the "truly marvelous proof" to your last theorem?!

You are teaching a Yale course. What is it called? (35 words or fewer)

A Deep Learning Approach to Analyze the Spanish Language

Most first-year Yale students live in suites of four to six people. What would you contribute to the dynamic of your suite? (35 words or fewer)

An inventive spirit: I make lotion, card games, 3D printed puzzles, and even words. Maybe my suitemates and I will experience blitzentente—the feeling that you deeply understand someone you just met.

Reflect on your engagement with a community to which you belong. How do you feel you have contributed to this community? (250 word limit)

It was sophomore year, and I had just started the 3D Design Club. I jumped up and down at club fair, holding a flamboyant sign in one hand and a 3D printed prosthetic hand in the other. "Join the 3D Design Club!" I shouted.

But I didn't just want to create a club. I wanted to create a community, a zone in between order and chaos where practicality and foolishness intertwine.

I try to coach members to be not only better designers but also better innovators. When members first design things, they tend to follow the rules, to stick to perceived notions of how something should look or work. So I show them a 3D printed puzzle cube I designed, but it is also a stationery organizer. You can open up each piece and put in staples, paper clips, and mechanical pencil lead. Throughout the three years of this club, I've seen members design everything from bookstands that curl up as a dragon's back to triangular marble mazes that grow upwards. To me, design is about empathy and human connection. We make inanimate objects. But we're making these objects for emotional, sentient human beings. The members of the club worked together to design a heart-shaped box for hospitalized patients; in every object, we add meaning by inscribing the recipient's name and engraving a quote or bible verse that relates to the recipient's situation. Today, my school has a community of designers, who now know how to turn their dreams into reality.

Write on something you would like us to know about you that you have not conveyed elsewhere in your application. (250 word limit)

Pouring out my heart makes me feel alive.

Speaking to an audience about a subject I am passionate about is one of the most meaningful experiences I have ever had. On my feet, while I pepper my sentences with humor when the atmosphere feels tense or lower my voice to emphasize a point, everything fades, and it is just the audience and me. I do not speak to tell people what to do. I speak in order to share my perspective, to start a conversation.

Ultimately, no matter how passionate I am with pathos or reasonable I am with logos, I cannot make people walk the extra ten feet to recycle or turn off the light after everyone else leaves the room. I can only encourage them to care. So I create moments with the audience: I pause, look them in the eye a little longer than I am supposed to, and suddenly, a strong, unexplainable connection is created. These brief moments, I believe, allow my points to resonate with the audience.

After my talk, people begin to discuss my arguments. Members of the audience come up to me and ask questions ranging from, "What steps should I take to start an environmental club at my school?" to "What should I do about my son's video game addiction?"

To speak is to step into the unknown, to create moments in which connection is created, in hopes that my words kindle passion.

If you selected one of the computer science or engineering majors, please tell us more about what has led you to an interest in this field of study, what experiences (if any) you have had in computer science or engineering, and what it is about Yale's program in this area that appeals to you. (Please answer in 500 words or fewer.)

"You're literally killing your laptop," my roommate pointed out. Figuratively, she was right: the powerful whir of the fans did little to cool the scorching laptop.

"But, I'll have answers. And a working search engine," I smiled.

My sophomore year, I conducted research on the convergence of a very elegant algorithm: PageRank, used by Google to determine the order of web pages. Does representing teleportation—the act of jumping to a completely new webpage—through modifying the matrix values by a dampening factor allow the PageRank algorithm to converge faster than through adding an extra node that points to, and is pointed to by, every other page? How does the dampening value affect convergence? Power method or Jacobi method? These questions buzzed around my mind. I was thinking about this algorithm while weaving through the art booths at the Des Moines Art Festival, turning PageRank over and over again in my head until it buried itself deep in my bones. I suddenly realized the whole scene looked like the way I envisioned the Internet: visitors as web surfers, jumping from one web page to the next and booths as web pages enticing visitors with curiosity-satiating content. As I watched the irregular, multi-directional movements of the human traffic, I wondered if using random initial values instead of the standard 1/n initial value could reduce convergence time, too.

That night, I sat next to the glowing, overheated laptop in the dark, eagerly waiting the answer to my hypothesis.

The way the right algorithm can solve seemingly impossible problems with only a few lines of code never ceases to intrigue me. Robert Sedgewick's book, *Algorithms*, was my bible as I self-studied concepts such as Dijkstra's algorithm and Minimum Spanning Trees. Discovering Dynamic Programming completely opened up my world: the recursive solution of finding the nth term of the fibonacci sequence is elegant already, but Dynamic Programming solves that and similar problems in linear time rather than in exponential time!

My dream is to use algorithms to improve medicine, such as creating an algorithm that can accurately predict life-threatening heart attacks or an algorithm that can repurpose existing drugs to treat other conditions, which will reduce drug development costs and consequently make drugs more affordable. Yale will best help me solve hitherto unimagined problems because it offers an unparalleled, liberal arts education with a brilliant student body and an emphasis on undergraduate research. With an education of both breadth and depth, I can delve into the human condition in English 123, and I can also immerse my engineering and entrepreneurial side as I perform algorithmic research through the Freshman Summer Research Fellowship, collaborate with students to design future medical devices at CEID, and launch a start-up with guidance from CITY. At Yale, my eyes will be opened again and again, not only when I am studying algorithms with world-renowned professors, but also when I am conversing with the interesting, service-oriented, and passionate student body.

ANALYSIS OF MY APPLICATION

I believe my acceptance letters were based on two key factors: 1) my academic profile, based on my transcript and standardized test scores, and 2) the duality of my tech/business side and writing/speaking side. As I applied with an entrepreneurial tilt, the presentation of this duality worked for me. Technology-based entrepreneurship, I believe, requires all those skills—an understanding of technology, a knack for business, and the ability to write, speak, and lead. The presence of this duality alone did not get me in, however. Rather, it was the depth of this duality, the meaningful accomplishments I carried in many disparate fields, that got me in. Ultimately, I believe I was not admitted for a specific talent. If they wanted to, they could probably fill an entire class with students far better in debate, writing, and computer programming than I am. However, what I demonstrated was a unique kind of versatility.

Here is a list of factors, ranked from most to least impactful, that I believe most influenced my acceptance into top-tier universities. The synergy of these factors showed that I was a top candidate.

1. Academic Profile
2. USACO Platinum Division
3. Chair of Youth Commission (Through Teens' Eyes)

4. Two summers of research
5. Business awards
6. Speech + debate awards
7. Essays

Despite the many strengths of my application, it was not perfect. I believe one strength of my application simultaneously acted as a weakness, that because I was involved in extracurriculars in so many different fields I failed to be world-class at anything. For example, while I spent two summers doing research, I did not win any major science fairs, and, while I earned many debate awards, I was not the Tournament of Champions winner. By involving myself in many disparate activities, I did not devote enough time and energy on any one of them to become exceptional.

The fact that my strength is simultaneously a weakness demonstrates that there is no one right approach to college admissions. What may work for one university may not work for another, and what may work for one admission officer may not work for another. What is true is that one must be impressive in their own unique way.

ANALYSIS OF MY ESSAYS

On a scale of 1 - 5, I would give my essays a 4. While they are not extraordinary, they do give admission officers a sense of who I am and why I do the activities that I do.

One of the strengths of my essays is how cohesive they are in showing specific aspects of my personality. For example, almost all my major essays show my commitment towards connecting with other people. Here is a list of areas from my Stanford application that shows this:

- The Common Application Essay: "In order to create a safe space where teens can write about their experiences without fear of judgement, I started the Through Teens' Eyes Project as a Youth Commissioner. I hoped that readers, young and old, would feel the depth of teens' humanity through these breathing stories."
- Roommate Essay: "i know this is quite antiquated—the whole fountain pen on card in an envelope thing, but i'm a huge fan of snail mail: the letters seem more meaningful..." The connection between this line and my desire to connect with other people is more subtle, but it is there. I show that I prefer handwritten letters because they speak to the reader more.
- Roommate Essay: "maybe we'll experience blitzentente (n.)—the feeling that you deeply understand someone you just met." Blitzentente is a word I made up, and the

meaning of this word shows that understanding other people is important to me.

- Speaking Essay: "So I create moments with the audience: I pause, look them in the eye a little longer than I am supposed to, and suddenly, a strong, unexplainable connection is created. These brief moments, I believe, allow my points to resonate with the audience."
- Speaking Essay: "To speak is to step into the unknown, to create moments in which connection is created, in hopes that my words kindle passion."
- Name one thing you are looking forward to experiencing at Stanford Essay: "Learning and designing solutions to world-wide problems at the d.school. Here, in between order and chaos, in the orientation-less rooms teeming with empathy, collaboration, and interdisciplinary study, I can apply my knowledge of computer science and mechanical engineering to develop novel solutions to social problems." In this short essay, I imply that I believe empathy is an important part of designing products.

As you can see, my desire to create bonds with other people is expressed throughout many of the essays I sent to Stanford. In fact, my Stanford admission officer mentioned how she was touched by my commitment towards forming bonds with others in her handwritten letter to me. In this way, my essays illuminate an aspect of my character that my transcript or extracurricular activities cannot. This thread of my desire to connect with others runs through my essays for MIT and Yale as well.

There are other threads, too. In my essays, I show the admission officers that I have an inventive spirit. See if you can find instances in my essays where that shines through.

Ultimately, these threads do not have to be explicitly stated. They can be described in the most subtle ways, and I think that is when they are the most powerful.

PART TWO:

Insights

EXTRACURRICULAR ACTIVITIES

What are top-tier universities looking for when reviewing your extracurricular activities?

Top-tier universities are looking for something impressive, something that shows there is something extraordinary about the applicant. This can take many forms, ranging from starting a successful business to writing beautiful essays unlike any they have read before. I believe there are three main methods for having stand-out extracurricular activities: personal projects, leadership, and high achievement.

What are personal projects, and why should I do them?

I believe one of the best things one can do for college applications and more importantly for one's growth is to embark on personal projects. Personal projects are self-designed projects one does outside of academics and traditional extracurricular activities. They require a spoonful of creativity and a pot-full of determination. Examples of personal projects include publishing a book, releasing a pop album, hitchhiking across the country, starting a blog, organizing a conference, building a mechanical device for your room, and starting a business or nonprofit. The possibilities are endless.

The beauty of personal projects comes from the fact that it's all your own. You see the project from the start to finish. There is a certain joy that comes from setting your heart on accomplishing something and seeing it through, a joy that comes from touching the creation of something that came from you. I believe our lives are already filled with personal projects, both big and small, ranging from cooking our favorite meals to reorganizing the house to even raising kids. Projects help fulfill us in some way or the other.

Personal projects can vary in size and scope, but I hope every high school student gets the chance to complete a project that seems slightly out of reach, a project that requires effort, a project with obstacles along the way. It will only make the victory all the more sweeter, the journey all the more richer. Additionally, a challenging project demonstrates grit, passion, and a willingness to make mistakes and to try even when there are no guarantees. The stories that can come out of persevering through personal projects can enrich essays. They can make an application come to life. On the other hand, a project that you can do with your eyes closed may not have the same effects.

For instance, the Through Teens' Eyes Project, while done through the Youth Commission, was a personal project for me because I was with the project from start to finish: I came up with the idea, pitched it, executed it, and held the completed product in my hands.

There were many hurdles along the way. I heard many "no's." At times, doors were slammed in my face. But with the help of an amazing team, I did it. This project has helped my application in many ways: I emphasized it during my college interviews, and my Common Application essay was centered around it. In fact, the Through Teens' Eyes project was one of the first things my Stanford admission officer wrote to me about in my acceptance letter and talked to me about when I met her in person. It is clear that it was one of the major factors of my acceptance.

I came up with the project because I enjoy stories, I am curious about the lives of those around me, and not just the rosy bits but the hard ones too, and I want to take in the rich diversity of my city. I tell you this because I know it can be hard to come up with a worthwhile project or to decide on a personal project to undertake. However, remember there is no objective answer. No project is better than the other. Instead of looking externally for a project, one must look within. Projects are a reflection of sorts of who you are and who and what you love.

Perhaps there has always been something itching inside your heart, but it has always seemed just beyond your reach. Perhaps there is something small tingling inside your chest but it is not big enough for you to act on. Perhaps there is something you want to understand, learn, or explore. Do not worry about having a "big passion" because, truthfully, many high school students do not have one. But many high school students do have little sparks, little passions, little dreams. Sometimes they are so little we are not aware of them, shut down as they are because of societal or parental expectations, inertia, or the lack of faith in oneself. I hope that with some introspection you begin to listen to the tiny inklings that beat in your blood. These tiny inklings do not have to be for a particular subject or extracurricular activity. Rather, they can be for a hobby, a person, a community, a language, a culture, a city, a feeling, an experience. And I would not worry about picking a project that is in a field that is "college application worthy." For instance, a project on video games can be just as unique and powerful as any other.

You may ask, "What if I have a good idea, but it seems hard to do?" I would say that creating something that adds value is never easy. That's why it can be a game-changer to your college application. The more meaningful and harder it is to pull off the project, the more it helps your application. For example, getting a book published by one of the "Big 5" publishing companies is extremely difficult, especially for a high school student, and that is why it is so *wow* on your application. Embarking on any personal project, regardless of the size or scope, is not easy.

Here are a couple of tips: 1) Reach out for help. Perhaps you can reach out to a teacher. You can also partner up with someone whose skills complement yours. Seek resources that can help you. 2) Plan to spend a lot of time and energy on your project. As I was embarking on my own personal projects, I often underestimated the time it would take, because while the projects seemed simple on the surface, there were a lot of details to work through underneath. Go in with the understanding that you are creating something from the ground-up and that you have to set enough time aside to do it well. 3) Take it one step at a time. It is okay to go slow, one foot after the other. Thinking of the end-goal might be daunting, but if you break the entire task into digestible parts, it will be easier. 4) Lastly, believe in yourself. Your faith in yourself will help you through many of the obstacles that come your way.

    I believe that any project, regardless of size or scope, is meaningful and can add vitality to your college applications. I always had a bias that I had to do something big. Because of this, I ignored all the smaller, meaningful projects that I wanted to accomplish in high school, such as starting a small tutoring business or learning how to create simple apps. Ultimately, everything big starts from someplace small. You never know how a small tutoring business can blossom into a huge one, or how a small app can segue into one used by millions. You never know how that one book you wrote that no publisher wanted can lead you to write the next bestseller. So go after big projects and go after small projects and enrich your summers and school years with not just one project but multiple, and in this way both discover and create who you are.

You mention high achievement can be an avenue through which one stands out through extracurricular activities. What if I am not talented in anything?

First—that is probably because you are thinking of the kinds of activities that take years to reach a high level, the kinds of activities that you must start as a young child to be world-class at, such as sports or music. If you start gymnastics as a freshman in high school, it will be extremely difficult for you to reach a recruitable level by junior or senior year.

But there are so many other activities you can pursue. For instance, photography. Even if you have never picked up a camera before, you can cultivate talent in photography if you dedicate time. With constant dedication, you could have a stunning photography portfolio and a vibrant photography business on the side.

For instance, as a freshman, I was a dismal debater. I was losing more than winning at tournaments in the novice division. Back then, I would never have believed that I would be ranked 23rd in the nation two years later.

My point is, for many activities, your dedication matters a lot more than your starting point. While I believe this is an easy concept to understand, I believe it is hard to fully internalize. In high school, I saw how talented students in my class were in drawing, tennis, debate, and math, and I therefore thought that these activities had no room for me. I wish I believed the quote I heard years later at Stanford, that "a large slope can beat out any y-intercept." Rather than focusing on where you are lacking, focus on where you want to go and who you want to become.

How do I pick an activity if I am not passionate about anything?

If you are interested in something, go after it, and do not worry if you are "passionate" about it yet. Passion is not something you stumble across—it is something that you cultivate over time, over years of familiarizing yourself with something and understanding its complexities. If you have an interest that comes from the heart and the understanding that dedication can propel you to success, the whole world is open to you.

Make sure your extracurricular activities substantiate one another.

It is important that, as a whole, your extracurricular activities work together to paint a picture of who you are. For example, through holding a high leadership position in government, starting my own city-wide project, and starting my own club, I showed the admission officers my ability to lead. That, alongside my awards in business and debate, allowed me to show admission officers that I could be a successful businesswoman in the future—one who can lead and talk persuasively. Do you see how all those activities came together?

My advice is to make sure that there is some cohesive thread that runs through multiple activities. For example, mentioning that your stock portfolio has increased by 200% is not extremely significant by itself. However, mentioning that you took finance classes at your local community college, started an investing club at your school, and won DECA competitions in the finance category on top of growing your stock portfolio by 200% is powerful. A chain of involvements shows depth. Having multiple activities support one another to tell a story of who you are and what your interests are is very compelling. Additionally, it is okay to have some activities dangle on the side, unrelated to your thread, like tennis in my case, because it shows you are willing to immerse yourself in other areas.

How many different activities should I do?

Here are some things you should know:

- Quality is better than quantity.
- It is okay to join a lot of activities, but be serious about a couple of them. For example, I joined some low-commitment lunch clubs that barely made my application, if at all. I joined them simply because my friends were there and because I wanted a place to hang out during lunch.

- My advice is to join many activities during your freshman year. Explore. See what you like. And narrow it down for sophomore year. Remember, it is okay to quit. At the beginning of my freshman year, I thought robotics would be my thing. I thought I would spend all four years doing it and that I would find my community there. But after spending so much time on it, I quit because I realized that spending time on something that I do not enjoy is a waste of time.

Should I fill out all 10 spots for extracurricular activities on the Common Application?

You do not have to fill out all 10 spots on the Common Application, nor do the admission officers expect you to. It is okay to leave some blank. Also, it might be beneficial for you to split the same activity into two or three sections if you have room. For example, if you did a special project as part of the robotics team, you could list that separately, or if you organized a conference as part of a club, you could list that conference separately as well. For example, I did some speaking engagements as part of the youth commission, and I listed that separately.

In the same vein, you do not need to fill out all 5 spots in the awards section. And please do not feel bad if you cannot. Let your impressiveness shine through in other ways.

Does being on a sports team help my application for top-tier universities?

Yes, if you are at a recruitable level, and yes if you are captain. If you are neither of those, being on a sports team will still help your application because it shows that you can dedicate significant time and energy towards something that you like. At the same time, however, while I believe simply being a part of a sports team will help your application, I do not believe that it will be a game-changer to your application. Just think of the number of people in your high school who play varsity sports and multiply that by the thousands of high schools in the US, and you'll see why it will not help your application significantly.

I also want to add that, in general, being a part of a sports team requires significant time and dedication. For example, I spent fifteen hours a week playing tennis during tennis season.

My advice is to play the sport if you intend to be highly accomplished in the sport or if you are highly passionate about it. Allowing your passion for a sport to shine through can color your application. I would advise not to play a sport if you are doing it simply for college applications; in that case, dedicating your time elsewhere would be more beneficial for you.

What should I do during the summer?

Lots of things! You could take college classes, start a project, participate in summer programs, etc. Think of the summer as ample time to strengthen your extracurricular activities. Many people believe that you need to participate in a structured summer program or get an internship or a job to have a "successful" summer for college applications. While those structured activities certainly boost your application, they are not the only productive ways to use your summer. Solo backpacking the Pacific Crest Trail, traveling to Spain to create a documentary about Spanish culture, taking care of your siblings, and creating your own t-shirt business are also impressive activities that would look great on a college application.

Is participating in a summer program useful?

How useful a summer program is really depends on the program and what you do in it. I will say, though, that *most* summer programs, while good experiences, will not be game-changers to your application to highly selective universities. For example, while COSMOS (a residential, four-week summer program in STEM at one of the UC campuses) will improve your application for UCs, it will not help you too much in getting into elite universities. However, it can be used as a stepping stone to get into more highly-selective, prestigious summer programs. And it can be a way to gain experience. My general advice is to do the program if it is interesting to you. Here is a list of highly prestigious summer programs that will contribute meaningfully to your application.

1. **Research Science Institute (RSI)** - Free, eight-week research program at MIT. RSI is one of the most prestigious research programs out there. I personally know many RSI alums at Stanford. For rising seniors.
2. **Stanford Institutes of Medicine Summer Research Program (SIMR)** - Eight-week research program at Stanford with a $500 stipend. Highly selective, with an acceptance rate of around 6%. For rising seniors or rising college freshmen.
3. **NIH Summer Internship Program in Biomedical Research (SIP)** - Eight to twelve week research program at the National Institutes of Health. For students of all education levels, including high school, college, and grad school.
4. **Telluride Association Summer Program (TASP)** - Great if you are interested in the humanities. Free, six-week program that focuses on discussion-based seminars, filled with readings, writing assignments, and intellectual community. Very distinguished faculty from top universities teach at TASP. Highly selective with an

intensive application process that involves numerous essays and an interview. For rising seniors.

Of course, these programs are not necessary to get into top universities. I list them here so that you are aware of them, and if they spark your interest, go search them up and apply.

What are some good competitions I should know about?
Here are competitions that might interest you.

- **Olympiads**: Olympiads are academic contests that test your critical thinking and problem-solving abilities. These contests are usually arranged by levels, where if you get a certain score on one level, you qualify to take a test for a higher level. Olympiads are very prestigious. Even passing one level is considered a big accomplishment. There are Olympiads in various subjects. If you are passionate about any of these subjects, I highly recommend you checking out the respective Olympiad.
  - *Math* (USA Mathematical Olympiad): You may recognize the name of the first exam—AMC. Typically, tenth-grade students and below take the AMC 10, and juniors and seniors take the AMC 12.
  - *Computer Programming* (USA Computing Olympiad): If you have taken AP Computer Science, I highly recommend you try this Olympiad out. With some practice, you should be able to pass the first level. There

93

are four levels: bronze, silver, gold, and platinum. Making it to the gold or platinum level is very prestigious. You can take the exam on your home computer.
- *Biology* (USA Biology Olympiad)
- *Chemistry* (USA Chemistry Olympiad)
- *Linguistics* (NACLO): This does not require additional knowledge of languages. I would highly recommend NACLO for those who like to solve puzzles and are fairly good at math.
- **Scholastic Arts & Writing** You should definitely submit to this contest if you like to write or create art. Thousands of students receive recognition at the local level. If you are very good, you can also get recognized at the national level. It is really not that hard to get recognized. Go give it a shot!
- **Entrepreneurship Competitions**: If you are interested in entrepreneurship, check out these pitch competitions: The Diamond Challenge, LaunchX, Columbia University Model Entrepreneur Competition, and DECA. These competitions give you the opportunity to come up with a business plan and pitch it to a panel of judges.
- **Science Fair:** If you have done research at a summer program or at school, check out these science fair competitions: Regeneron Science Talent Search, Siemens Competition, Google Science Fair. If you have done

research in the arts, social sciences, or humanities, check out MIT Inspire.

What if I am interested in research, but did not get into any summer research programs?

My advice would be to email many professors at universities near you. I have never done this, but some of my friends have—and were successful. In the email, attach a resume and explain why you want to do this particular field of research and what skills you have. Generally, you have to email tens of professors, and hopefully one will say yes.

And again, doing research is not necessary to get into the tippy-top schools. Do not think you have to do it because everyone else around you is doing it. But if you are genuinely interested in research, email the professors.

Should I start a club at my school?

Absolutely! It teaches you how to lead and to run an organization. It shows colleges that you have initiative and leadership. Again, starting a club is not necessary for getting into elite universities, but in my opinion, it is a great learning experience.

Steps to starting a club:
1. Come up with the kind of club you want to start
2. Come up with the kinds of activities members of the club will do during the meetings (ex. give presentations, organize events, organize fundraisers, do hands-on projects)
3. Recruit some of your classmates to be leaders of the club
4. Approach a teacher to advise the club
5. Pick a meeting time and location
6. Register the club with the school to make it official
7. Post flyers around the school and have a booth at club fair
8. Collect the names and emails of prospective members, and email them to remind them to come to the club meetings
9. (Optional) Design club t-shirts that members of your club can buy to raise funds for the club
10. (Optional) Organize a bake sale to raise funds for the club

What kind of club should I start?

Anything, really. Some examples are astronomy club, book club, anime club, puzzle club, marine biology club, pre-med club, green energy solutions club, etc. The possibilities are endless!

What is important at the end of the day?

At the end of the day, it does not matter what extracurricular activities you engage in. The important thing is to demonstrate genuine drive, passion, and talent. Be impressive.

ACADEMICS

What is the most important part of the application?

Your transcript is arguably the most important part of your application. This document shows your course load, grades, and GPA, and is used to calculate your class rank.

What GPA should I aim for?

GPA calculation varies between high schools, as many high schools use different GPA scales and have different GPA policies. Additionally, academic rigor varies drastically from school to school. Because of these reasons, it is very difficult to give a set bar you should aim for.

Most colleges such as Stanford and Yale (but not MIT) evaluate applications by region, meaning that there is an admission officer assigned to your specific region. As a result, all the applications from the same region and therefore the same school will be read by the same admission officer. The admission officer reading your application will have a general idea of how GPA is calculated, what classes are offered, and the overall academic rigor at your high school.

This has several implications. First, if your school has a funky way of calculating GPA, you do not need to worry. Second, the admission officer is looking at your GPA and overall course load in relation to the other applicants who applied from your school; therefore, instead of focusing on how high your GPA should be, focus instead on your class rank (or if your school does not rank students, focus on being in the top echelon of students).

What is class rank, and why is it important? What class rank should I aim for?

Class rank is a measure of how your GPA compares to that of the other students in your grade. Some schools give an explicit class rank (ex. #1). Other schools give percentages (ex. top 5%). And others do not rank at all.

If your school does rank students, you will most likely be asked to report your class rank. The class rank gives admission officers a way of determining how you compare academically to your peers.

You should aim to be in at least the top 10%. Being in the top 5% or top 1% is better.

If I get a B, is my life over?!?!?

Aim for A's, of course! Getting one or two B's—especially in areas that you are not planning on majoring in—is not going to eliminate you. It is not ideal, but it is okay. I know plenty of people who got into Stanford who have B's on their application. Generally, getting one or two B's is okay. It may hurt your application to some extent, but I do not think it will hurt your application significantly. But getting a lot of B's or a C is definitely very detrimental.

At the end of the day, it is all relative. If you are an Olympic gold medalist in ice skating or the best debater in the country, you can afford to get more B's than, say, someone like me.

Aim for A's. Not A-'s. But A's. If you miss, that is okay. The doors of every top university are still open for you.

How can I make my transcript stand out?

You do not need a transcript that stands out. Rather, you only need a transcript that is good enough—one that shows you are academically competent and are challenging yourself. However, having a transcript that stands out can boost your admission chances. Here are some suggestions:

1. <u>Take multiple languages.</u> Taking at least two different languages a year differentiates you, especially if you get to the AP level in all of them. If you really like to learn languages, you can always study over the summer to skip a level.
2. <u>Take college classes.</u> You can take classes at your local community college. Take classes that interest you and are not offered at your high school, such as high-level math, creative writing, and neuroscience. Schools like Stanford allow high school students to take classes in their summer quarter.

What is AP?

Advanced Placement is a program spearheaded by College Board that offers college-level courses for high school students. For each AP class, there is an exam offered at the end of the year, scored on a scale of one through five. A score of three or above is considered a passing score. The percentage of students receiving each score varies drastically between AP exams.

Additionally, not every school is part of the AP program. Some schools are part of the IB program instead, or are a part of neither. If your school does not offer any AP classes, please disregard the advice pertaining to AP listed below.

How many AP classes should I take?

You should take as many as you can while still maintaining top grades in all classes and still leaving time for both enough sleep and your other involvements.

In addition, colleges focus on five different areas when they look at your transcript: math, science, English, history, and foreign language. As a general rule of thumb, you should reach the AP level (or the highest level your school offers) for four out of five of these areas.

There is no hard and fast rule for the number of AP classes you should take. Remember that colleges are looking at your course load in part to make sure that you are taking advantage of the opportunities your high school provides—in this case, your high school's classes. Colleges want to make sure that, if admitted, you will take full advantage of the resources available to you at their institution. In general, whether your school offers AP or IB or neither, make sure you take advantage of the classes offered.

A note on picking classes

A lot of people have anxiety over picking classes. They wonder *should I add AP Environmental Science for the extra AP? Should I take AP Physics 1 or AP Econ or both?* I believe that as long as you are positioning yourself to be one of the top students in your class and as long as you are taking a pretty rigorous course load, the minute details do not matter as much. Ultimately, admission officers are trying to answer one question: will this student thrive academically at this university?

Should I take the AP exam? Do I have to report my AP scores?

The AP exam is not mandatory, and some students choose not to take the AP exam after taking the AP class. Many students do not take the AP exam because they assume that they will get a low score. However, most universities do not require an official AP score report for the application reviewing process. Instead, AP scores are self-reported. On most college applications, there is a space on the application where you can list your AP scores. You do not need to report all your scores. In general, you should report scores of three or higher and leave out scores of two or lower.

This means a bad score will not hurt you in the sense that colleges do not have to see it. Because of this, I recommend you take the AP exam. Being scared of a bad score should not be a reason not to take the AP exam. You should also remember that AP exams are not designed for you to get perfect raw scores. Therefore, even getting a raw score of 50% could get you a three or higher depending on the exam.

It is also important to note that colleges will know if you choose not to report your AP score or if you do not take the AP exam; they can compare the AP classes on your transcript to the AP scores you reported. Not taking AP exams even though you took the respective AP classes could be a red flag on your application. Colleges would assume you did not report your scores because you got bad ones or because you were not confident enough to take the exam. It will not hurt your application significantly if you left out one score but anything more than that could concern admission officers.

How important are AP scores, really?

AP scores matter—but their importance certainly pales in comparison to the other aspects of your application. For example, your transcript and SAT or ACT score are more important. That being said, a string of 5's is certainly impressive. It shows the admission officers that you have a firm grasp of college-level material, and it demonstrates your academic competency. If you go to a relatively easy high school where A's are not hard to come by, getting high AP scores could be a way of differentiating yourself from your peers.

On the other hand, getting mediocre or bad AP scores can severely hurt your application for highly selective universities. Getting many 3's and some 2's tells admission officers that you are not fully grasping the material, and they could call into question your ability to survive academically at a selective university. In addition, for highly selective colleges, getting one or two 5's, many 4's, and some 3's is not ideal, but it definitely will not eliminate you.

It is important to remember that quality is better than quantity when it comes to AP classes. Taking a few AP classes and doing well on all the exams is better than taking many AP classes but not doing well on the exams.

Should I self-study AP courses outside of school?

Some people, in an effort to boost the competitiveness of their application, take additional AP exams without taking the respective AP class. Usually, they will pick a relatively easier AP, such as AP Environmental Science or AP Psychology, buy an AP prep book, and self-study the AP exam.

I did not self-study any AP courses outside of school, nor do I think it helps your application significantly. As mentioned previously, AP exam scores are already not so important compared to the other aspects of your application, so I do not advise doing this in most situations. It would be much better if you spend your time doing extracurriculars or focusing on getting top grades.

However, self-study AP exams if you cannot enroll in a good number of AP classes in your sophomore or junior years of high school. For example, if you are unable to take any AP classes your sophomore year, you should consider self-studying one or two APs. If you do this, I would advise you to choose a more substantial AP test, like AP Biology and AP English Language.

Additionally, if you are fluent in another language, I would recommend taking the AP exam for that respective language. It will show the admission officers that you are competent in another language.

What are the best resources for preparing for AP exams?

Here are a couple of resources that I used to study for AP exams:

1. <u>College Board Website</u>: College Board releases past AP exams. Sometimes, the practice tests in AP prep books do not capture the true feel and difficulty level of the exam, so the past AP exams on the College Board website are the best way to prepare. AP tests are divided into two sections: the multiple-choice section and the free-response section. Generally, College Board releases many free-response sections but does not release many multiple-choice sections, so please use the multiple-choice practice tests resourcefully.

2. <u>AP Pass Score Calculator</u>: The AP Pass Score Calculator gives you a general sense of how well you need to do on the exam to earn a certain score. For example, using an AP Pass Score Calculator, you know that if you get around a 70% on the multiple-choice section of the AP English Language exam and 7/9 on all three essays, you should be at the threshold for a 5. Remember that these score calculators are not 100% accurate because the AP exam is graded on a curve, and the curve could change year to year.

3. <u>AP Prep Books:</u> AP prep books are helpful in two ways. First, they refresh your memory on certain concepts you may have forgotten. Second, they give you practice questions. As mentioned earlier, the AP books' practice tests might not accurately reflect the difficulty level or the feel of the real AP exam, but doing the practice questions is still helpful. Generally, the Baron's prep book is known to be harder than the actual exam, and the Princeton Review prep book is known to be easier than or at the same level of the actual exam. This is not true for all of the AP exams, but it seems to be the case from my past experience. Usually, I used both the Baron's and the Princeton Review prep books to study for AP exams.

What are the SAT II Subject Tests?

SAT II Subject Tests are one-hour tests on specific subjects. There are 20 different SAT II Subject Tests: Math Level 1, Math Level 2, Biology E/M, Chemistry, Physics, English Literature, U.S. History, World History, and an assortment of different language exams. A perfect score on SAT II Subject Tests is an 800.

Think of SAT II Subject Tests like AP exams. While the SAT II Subject Tests are much shorter than AP exams, they are made by the same company, so the material covered on both exams is similar. For example, after I took the AP US History exam my junior year, I took the SAT II Subject Test for US History, and, because I already studied for the AP exam, I did not study much for the SAT II Subject Test.

SAT II Subject Tests are different from the actual SAT, and you cannot take SAT II Subject Tests the same day you take the actual SAT. You can, however, take multiple SAT II Subject Tests on the same day.

Do I need to take SAT II Subject Tests?

Colleges vary greatly on their policy towards SAT II Subject Tests. Because these policies change relatively frequently, I encourage you to check with each school you are planning to apply to. As of now, most colleges either recommend them or consider them, and a few colleges require them. Because of this, I recommend taking two SAT II Subject Tests. If you are planning on majoring in something in the STEM field, I recommend taking the SAT II Math Level 2 exam. For highly selective colleges, I believe a score of 760 or higher on SAT II Subject Tests is ideal.

Should I take the SAT or the ACT?

Rest assured that colleges look at the SAT and ACT equally, so which test you take depends on your preferences. My advice is to not try to take them both. It is okay to take a practice test for both the SAT and ACT to see which one is better for you, but do not try to study for both tests at once. It is not time efficient. Choose one and stick to it. Here are some considerations:

1. The ACT has four sections: Math, Science, English, and Reading. The SAT has two: Evidence-Based Reading and Writing, and Math. The main difference is that the ACT has a science section and the SAT does not. The Science section of the ACT does not require deep knowledge of science; rather it tests scientific skills such as reading graphs and charts, and analyzing scientific passages.
2. The SAT gives more time per question than the ACT does. When taking the ACT, you are put under a lot of time pressure. So if you are the type of person who reads slowly and spends a lot of time on test questions, the SAT is probably a better choice for you.
3. From my experience, the Reading section of the SAT is harder than the Reading section of the ACT—if you do not take the time constraints into account. In general, people who are more STEM-inclined have found the ACT to be easier because they are good at math and science and because the Reading section is easier.

How high does my ACT or SAT score need to be?

Your ACT or SAT score is important, much more important than your AP scores or SAT II scores. It is the most important standardized test in high school. While a strong ACT or SAT score cannot make up for a lousy GPA, it is a strong indicator of your academic competency for universities. It is hard for me to tell you a score you should aim for, especially because factors such as geographic region and race need to be taken into account. I believe, even for those belonging to the most competitive pool of applicants, a 35+ on the ACT or a 1560+ on the SAT is golden.

How much time should I spend studying?

I believe studying two to four hours a day is a good amount. If time studying is eating into extracurriculars and, more importantly, sleep, I recommend refining your study strategies. Efficiency is not something that is fixed or inherent to you; rather, efficiency is something that must be cultivated.

For instance, shifting from passive studying to active studying has been effective for me. While I spend time memorizing material, I spend most of my time trying to deeply understand the concepts. When I read from the textbook, I not only try to follow what is going on, but I also make sure the concepts make logical sense to me. If I have any questions, I will write them down.

Taking steps to improve focus has also proven to be effective for me. This includes turning off notifications on my phone while I study, finding a good study space, and working in twenty-five minute, focus-sharp bursts. Also, I have learned that scheduling is powerful. Try it.

I believe it is important to make efficient studying a priority. I have seen too many high school students stay up until 2:00 or 3:00 AM studying, and this is simply unsustainable. Learning how to study effectively is conducive to success, as it opens time for more vitality to enter your life.

RECOMMENDATION LETTERS

RECOMMENDATION LETTERS

Recommendation letters are a vital aspect of a college application. In my opinion, recommendation letters matter more than what people might expect. While heavily subjective, recommendation letters are able to show important qualities, such as the student's participation in the classroom and ability to impress faculty, and can offer concrete details and stories that reveal qualities that cannot be gleaned from the other components of the application. I believe that glowing recommendation letters can be big pluses, while lackluster recommendations can be detrimental.

Why are recommendation letters important?

While there is no mold for getting into top-tier universities, in general, they are seeking students who will contribute meaningfully to their campus and beyond. This can manifest itself in a variety of ways. For instance, universities seek students who are active in the classroom, students who ask insightful questions and contribute meaningfully to discussions. Universities are looking for students who are curious, students who constantly inquire about the world around them and challenge common thought. Universities desire students who are good to those around them, who are respectful and compassionate; in other words, students who will make good roommates. Universities want students who will engage with professors, who will help others when they need help, who will be good citizens. Universities are also trying to create a diverse class, filled with students of all different personality types.

Your transcript and extracurricular activities do little to say about your personality. As a result, admission officers will turn to your recommendation letters to gain some insight into how you interact with your teachers and your peers.

What makes an outstanding recommendation letter?

<u>Superlatives</u>: Consider this phrase, "Mel is the best student I have had in the my thirty years of teaching." Pretty impressive, right? Of course, it is very hard to be the best student in thirty years. Even the phrase, "best student this year" is very powerful. Other superlatives such as "one of the most creative thinkers I have stumbled across" or "one of the most compassionate people I have had a chance to teach" are glowing statements. You cannot control whether or not a teacher writes about you using superlatives, but I hope this gives you a sense of what top-quality recommendations look like.

<u>Concrete examples:</u> Broad strokes without details do not make for the best of recommendation letters. While sweeping statements such as, "she is curious," make the recommendation better, if they are unsupported by concrete examples, the admission officers may not completely buy it.

The juice of the recommendation letter comes from the details. The examples and stories the recommender tells about you are what elevate the letter. Imagine, instead, the recommender says, "She is curious. Every class, she asks insightful questions about the lecture, demonstrating a sharp mind restless for knowledge. For example, when I was lecturing about parametric equations, she asked me if 3D printers utilized parametric equations. Her questions keep the other students in class more engaged and interested."

Here is another example: "Every day when he walks into my classroom, I can count on his warm, confident smile. Every day, he asks me how my day is." Even something as simple as that can turn a mediocre recommendation into a great one. This should tell you that you can get a good recommendation just by the steady doing of small deeds that most other students do not do. Doing something as simple as saying hello to a teacher before each class or regularly asking questions will set you apart.

Do I need to have a good relationship with those who will write my recommendation letters?

Developing a good relationship with your teachers is important. If you are close to your teachers, they will know more about you and your story. Thus, they will be able to insert more concrete details, and more importantly they will be more invested in writing your letter of recommendation.

While it is important to have a good relationship with your teachers, it is not necessary. For example, I did not have a relationship with my AP US History teacher outside of the classroom, but I constantly asked questions in class and contributed to discussions. At the end of the year, he told me I was one of his top students.

However, I did have good relationships with other teachers who wrote my recommendation letters. For example, throughout high school, my business mentor guided me through business competitions and even traveled with me to international competitions. I asked her for a recommendation letter, and I believe that letter helped me get into top-tier universities.

Therefore, while it is not necessary to foster close relationships with every recommender, it is beneficial to be close to at least one teacher.

How do I form a good relationship with teachers?

Building a relationship takes time. Be patient, as it is not going to happen overnight. Think of a relationship as a plant: it is slow-growing and needs constant nourishment. You need to continue watering the plant. It is the accumulation of small, meaningful interactions that allows for your relationship to grow. Here are some simple suggestions:
- When you enter your teacher's classroom, say "good morning" or "good afternoon" with a smile every time. It is

not good enough to do it once or once in a while. Do it every time. It will make a difference.

- Come to class early and talk to your teachers. Be curious about their lives. Ask about their children, about why they decided to become teachers, about why they teach the subject that they do, about where they were raised, about their beliefs and dreams. They would be more than happy to answer. The key is to be *genuinely interested.*
- When the teacher asks you how you are doing, do not just answer with a simple "good." Add something. Share a little about yourself. It is okay to open up, too. It is okay to say that you had a rough day or are feeling stressed. Teachers want to know about the real you, not the perfect version of you.
- Thank your teachers. Just shouting, "Hey Mrs. Smith, loved that lecture today. Thank you!" before you leave the classroom makes a difference. Additionally, you should write your teachers a thank-you card at the end of each semester. On the thank-you card, be genuine. Do not write statements like "you changed my life" unless the teacher really has. The thank-you card has to feel authentic and true from your heart. Only then does it make a difference. To make your card feel more authentic, use specific examples. Is there anything the teacher said that stuck to you? What particular activities or lectures did you enjoy? The more specific you get, the more genuine the thank-you will feel.

Writing those thank-you cards takes time. I spent at least thirty minutes on each thank-you card because they were so important to me. I did not just write a few sentences here and there. I filled out the whole card, and I gave my teachers personalized gifts that I made myself.
- Be an active participant in class. Ask insightful questions, contribute to discussions meaningfully, and help others when they do not understand or are behind. The worst thing you can do is to sit in the back of the classroom and stay silent the whole time.
- Just be you. If you have something funny to say, say it. I joked around in class. I challenged my teachers. I was not perfect, as I said and did things I probably should not have said and done. But at the end of the day, my teachers knew me. And that made all the difference.

Wow, it must be hard to get a good recommendation letter.

It is not hard to get a good recommendation letter. It might be hard for a teacher to say, "this is the best student I had in thirty years," but it is not hard to get a recommendation letter worthy of top-tier universities. I've said this before, but I want to highlight it: *All it takes is the steady application of small acts that most students do not do.*

What does the recommendation form look like?

I am going to refer to the Common Application recommendation here, the recommendation form that most universities use. In addition to a free-for-all question that allows recommenders to write about whatever they think is important, there is a ratings section. In this section, recommenders are asked to rate your qualities such as "academic achievement," "intellectual promise," "quality of writing," "creative, original thought," "productive class discussion," "respect accorded by faculty," "disciplined work habits," "maturity," "motivation," "leadership," "integrity," "reaction to setbacks," "concern for others," "self-confidence," "initiative, independence" as "below average," "average," "good (above average)," "very good (well above average)," "excellent (top 10%)," "outstanding (top 5%)," or "one of the top few I've encountered (top 1%)."

For highly-selective schools, it is important that you are mostly in the top 5% or top 1% category.

How many recommendations do I need?

The number of recommendation letters you need depends on the university, but typically two teacher recommendations are required in addition to one from your high school counselor. You typically can ask additional teachers or outside adults such as sports coaches, managers, or research mentors to submit additional recommendation letters. Some schools, like MIT, do not have a limit on how many recommendations you can submit. My suggestion is to ask 2-3 teachers and 1-2 outside adults. Admission officers do not want to be reading 10 recommendations! Ultimately, do not submit an additional recommendation unless you believe it will truly add to your application. There is nothing wrong with having two strong recommendation letters in addition to your counselor recommendation. You will not have an advantage submitting an additional letter unless it is able to show another dimension of your character or is extremely glowing.

Any advice on which teacher I should ask?

You should ask the teacher who you think will write you the best recommendation. Note that this is not the same as the teacher who you think likes you the best. A teacher can like you but not know you well. Choose the teacher of the class that you participated the most in. Choose the teacher who you think has the most concrete details to back up what they write. Even if they do not remember those concrete examples, you can give them a document that explains them in depth.

Does it matter when the teacher taught me?

Typically, junior-year teachers are best because they have had one year to get to know you, and unlike sophomore-year teachers your interactions in the classroom are still fresh in their memory. That being said, it is perfectly okay to ask a teacher you had sophomore year. It is also okay to ask a senior-year teacher, although that is not ideal. If that is what you want to do, make sure you are really active in class first semester so that the senior-year teacher can get to know you better. I would shy away from freshman-year teachers for the two primary recommendations because it has been so long since they taught you, and colleges would prefer to have a more up-to-date report on how you are in the classroom. But it is perfectly okay for freshman-year teachers to be third recommenders.

Should I have one STEM recommendation and one humanities recommendation?

Some schools, such as MIT, require this. They require that you ask one teacher in the STEM field and one teacher in the humanities to write you a recommendation letter. Other schools do not care. It is preferable to have one STEM recommendation and one humanities recommendation, especially if you are a STEM major and are applying to liberal-artsy universities like Yale or Columbia. But remember, for schools that do not have this requirement, the content of the letter is way more important than the subject the recommender teaches.

When should I ask for a recommendation letter?
End of junior year is best. Early senior year (within the first two weeks of school) is also good. Give your recommenders time. The earlier you ask, the more time they have to write it.

What should I give my recommenders to help them write me a better recommendation?
I would recommend giving your recommenders a document that contains the following:
- The grade you received in the class
- An explanation of why you liked his or her class. What did you learned? How did you grow intellectually or personally through this class?
- A description of the meaningful ways you contributed to the class (ex. an insightful comment during a discussion, a thought-provoking question you posed to the teacher, a time when you helped a student)
- A description of a project you did in class that you are proud of
- Anything else you wish your teacher would mention

I know giving this type of document may seem pushy, but it will in fact make it significantly easier for your recommender.

ESSAYS

What is the Common Application essay?

On the Common Application, you are asked to write an essay between 250 - 650 words. This essay is sent to every school that uses the Common Application. The Common Application essay is meant to be very open-ended, meaning you can write almost anything you want.

Because the essay prompts are so open-ended, my advice would be to ignore the prompt initially. Simply write an essay about something that comes from your heart.

What other essays do I need to write, besides the Common Application essay?

Most schools will require you to write additional supplemental essays in addition to the Common Application essay. Each school varies in the amount and type of supplemental questions asked.

When should I start my essays?

Preferably, you should start your essays the summer before senior year. This will give you ample time to write your essays before the early application deadline in November and the regular application deadline in January.

What topic should I write my essay on?

It really does not matter. Your essay topic does not have to be major-related. For example, I applied as a computer science major to most schools, yet my Common Application essay was about writing. The details make an essay good, not the topic. Use your topic as a vehicle to talk about something much deeper.

You do not need to write about big things or great achievements to have a good essay. Some of the best essays are about simple, ordinary things: walking to school, baking cookies, or biking around town. To see the extraordinary in the ordinary—that is special.

Is there anything I should not write about?

I would stay away from mentioning any awards you received in your essays because that is already listed in the application. It also could sound very boastful if not done right.

Why do my essays matter?

Your transcript, awards, extracurricular activities, and recommendation letters do not paint a full portrait of you. Admission officers want to know more: How do you see the world? What are the types of things you think about? What are your dreams? The essays humanize you. They add another dimension to your application beyond just the hard numbers. While the other aspects of your application tell admission officers what kind of student you are, the essays tell admission officers what kind of human you are. The essay gives your application a soul.

What makes a good essay?
1. Authenticity: The best essays are the ones that are authentic. Don't try to pretend like you are cooler, more funny, or more outgoing than you actually are. Write about the person you are, not about the ideal version of yourself. Write with your voice. The truth is your strength.
2. Reflection: All good essays show some reflection. It could be a reflection about yourself, about an activity, about culture, about nature, about philosophy, about anything really. Reflection is important because it reveals how you see the world and how you come to terms with it. The best kind of reflection reveals the subtleties and nuances of life. Please read the next section to better understand what reflecting looks like.
3. Anecdotes: Tell a story. Ground your story with specificity. Pull the reader in.
4. Good writing: This is an essay. Good essays are constructed by good writing. You do not have to be an extraordinary writer, but pay attention to your word choice and sentence structure. Most of these admission officers are not STEM majors—they are humanities

majors. Good, thoughtful, authentic, reflective writing appeals to them.

At the end of the day, there is no one way to write a college essay. There is no formula, no format you should follow. Just do you.

Help! I don't know how to start.

First, I would like to remind you that an essay is not supposed to represent the whole story of your life. It is impossible to capture all of who you are in 650 words. Therefore, your goal should be to offer the admission officers a glimpse of who you are. If you reorient your goal to that, the whole essay process will seem less daunting.

Second, just start writing. You can write about anything. The mere process of writing can get your creative juices flowing. Additionally, you cannot expect a perfect essay on your first draft. In fact, I wrote six different Common Application essays before I finally settled on an idea I wanted to pursue.

Third, I would recommend for you to think about your extracurricular activities and how you spend your free time. Really think about why you do what you do, and articulate that. For example, if you like photography, ask yourself why. What kinds of things do you like to take pictures of? What do you find aesthetic? Ask yourself questions and dig deep, and write your answers down. Here's an example that I came up with: *I like photography because I want to capture moments. That's why I like to take pictures of people mid-action. It is so that one day I can look back at those photos and remember the moments like they were yesterday—the texture, feel, and breath of them.* Here's another example: *I like to take photos of people staring directly into the camera, their face a reflection of their feelings. Some people are smiling. Others look stoic. Others look like they're in pain. And within each expression, there is always a subtlety somewhere—maybe it is the softness of one's dark blue eyes or a faint smile on a sad face—that makes me feel like I'm standing right in front of them, feeling what they are feeling.* If you are able to write a few sentences like that, you are off to great start. Just remember to keep digging. Keep asking why. Introspect.

How important are the essays?

To be honest, you may think essays are more important than they actually are. Because essays are the only things that can be controlled by senior year, people place a special emphasis on them. Essays are not as make-you-or-break-you as people think they are. That being said, very bad essays can hurt your application, and very great essays can give you a leg up. In general, if you have strong academics and strong extracurriculars, you do not need extraordinary essays to get you in. However, if you are lacking in other parts of your application or if you are on the borderline, having great essays can help you a lot.

When should I stop editing my essays?

The hardest part is not starting the essay but knowing when to stop. This is important because you are going to have to write many different essays, and you don't have enough time to edit them all to perfection. My advice would be to ask yourself these three questions: First, are you sure that there are no grammar mistakes? Second, does the essay genuinely reveal who you are? Third, are you proud of your essay? If your answer is yes to all three of these questions, I say you can stop editing that essay.

CONCLUSION

TO CONCLUDE, I would like to give you a concise and powerful list of insights, a kind of list I wish I had throughout high school. Most of the advice on this list you already heard before. I heard most of them, too, by the time I entered high school. However, I wish I had not only understood these snippets of advice but also internalized them, truly lived them out. I hope you internalize the ones you agree with, too. Some of these I've stated before; others are new. To me, they are all important.

1. College admissions is not about intelligence

The summer after my freshman year of college, I took a shuttle to go to work every weekday. One day, the driver looked at me through the front mirror. When I caught his gaze, he asked, "Where do you go to school?"

"Stanford," I said.

"Ah," he said. "You must be very smart then."

At the time, I could not find a satisfying reply to his comment, since his comment highlighted a major misconception about college admissions. I would like to undermine the common belief that there exists a causal relationship between intelligence and college admissions. I believe this misconception can be dangerous because underlying it is the belief that intelligence and therefore college admissions is fixed—the belief that if you are not the smartest person in the room, then a top-tier college is simply beyond reach.

While natural talent in a particular activity and an ability to learn quickly are helpful attributes, college admissions is about so much more. Confidence, maturity, determination, hard work, compassion, and courage are examples of other important attributes that can play just as significant or even more significant of a role in college admissions.

2. Have courage

Courage is an attribute that is rarely talked about in college admissions, yet I believe it is vital. Good things happen to people who are willing to put themselves out there—to those, for instance, who have the courage to try out for the varsity team even though they might not make the cut, to those who have the courage to try a new activity during high school, to those who have the courage to build a relationship with a teacher by going to office hours every week, to those who have the courage to embark on a project that may not work out, to those who have the courage to email dozens of professors for a research position, to those who have the courage to follow their heart despite knowledge of an easier, less-risky path. If I were to do high school all over again, it is this quality that I would continually remind myself of—for I believe it is absolutely foundational to succeeding uniquely and authentically.

3. It is okay if you do not have a passion

I believe the traditional advice of "follow your passion" does not work for many students entering high school. You cannot expect thirteen, fourteen, or fifteen year olds to all have a grand passion in life. Some will, and I think that's amazing! But I believe the majority are on a path towards discovery.

If you are one of these people, I encourage you to follow the little tugs in your heart, the inklings of interests that bubble within you. Do not worry about your interests being just a phase or not strong enough. If it intrigues you, I'd say go for it because if that activity is meant to be, the passion will come. As I said earlier in this book, passion is not something you stumble across —it is something that you cultivate over time, over the years of familiarizing yourself with something and understanding its complexities. So get started on the activities you are interested in, and maybe they will turn into passions.

4. The domino effect

Sometimes, getting into a top-tier university seems unreachable because the people who get in do all these amazing things that seem impossible. I certainly felt this way when I started high school. But just remember that all these amazing things can come to you, too. Remember that it is okay to start someplace small. If you actively grow step by step, you will see how one activity leads to another, how one accomplishment leads to a bigger one, how a single domino can create large-scale, lasting impact. So take it one domino at a time, and maybe one of those dominos down the line will be an acceptance letter to your dream university.

5. Getting into a top-tier university is not a shot in the dark

Based on the single-digit acceptance rates of top-tier universities, it would seem as if admission into these institutions is a shot in the dark.

The first step you need to take is to believe that getting into a top-tier university is something that is doable, something that relies on more than chance and luck. Based on Stanford's 4% acceptance rate, it may seem as if you have a 4% chance of getting into Stanford. This is simply not the case! You may actually have a much higher chance of getting in depending on your academics, extracurricular activities, recommendation letters, and essays.

6. Genuinely believe you can do it

Do not feel intimidated and think that getting into a top-tier university is impossible. If you ever come to Stanford, you will realize that the students there are regular teenagers—students just like you. So believe that getting into a top-tier university is doable if you put your heart to it, and just start small, work hard, take it one step at a time, and beautiful things will come. I hope I see you on the Stanford campus one day!

ACKNOWLEDGMENTS

I would like to thank everyone who has supported me over the years: my teachers for inciting curiosity, my classmates for the fun, classroom memories, and my parents for always having my back. The college admission process is not a solo journey, and I owe much gratitude to all whose paths have intersected with mine. I would like to especially extend a thank you to my friend David for designing the cover of this book and for his perspectives on life. Finally, I would like to thank my peers at Stanford for inspiring me in ways I did not know possible and for an incredible year. Here's to many more.

Contact:
harpertangbooks@gmail.com

Made in the USA
Las Vegas, NV
01 December 2021